QUANTUM MEMORY

Working Magic with Your Memory

by

Bobbi DePorter
with Mike Hernacki

Learning Forum Publications
Oceanside, California USA

D1010396

LEARNING FORUM PUBLICATIONS
1725 South Coast Highway
Oceanside, CA 92054-5319 USA
(760) 722-0072
(760) 722-3507 fax
email: info@learningforum.com
www.learningforum.com

Cover design by Kelley Thomas
Illustrations by Ellen Duris

ISBN: 0-945525-20-6

Dedicated to all the very special Learning Forum staff who over the years have contributed so much.

I acknowledge my son, Grant DePorter, for his contribution in the writing of Working Magic with Your Memory. *He uses memory techniques extensively in most areas of his life and has discovered distinctions and systems that improve other methods.*

Working Magic With Your Memory

? *Why is having a strong WIIFM especially important to memory?*

? *What two skills are the basis of memory improvement?*

? *What elements make information more memorable?*

? *What are the advantages to learning a memory system, like the Peg List?*

Contents

1

Motivation–The Key to Memory

Do you remember people's faces but not their names? Have you ever wished you could make your speeches more spontaneous-sounding and not have to constantly refer to your notes? Memory skills are important both for business and personal success, and through the years, experts have produced numerous books, tapes, and seminars about how to improve your memory. But just how well do these methods work? Will you even remember how to use them once you've completed the book or seminar? More importantly, will you be motivated to use them? And will knowing and using the skills have a significant impact on your life?

This book explains core memory skills—those that make the most difference. All the memory classes in the world won't help you in the least if what they teach doesn't fit your style. You must see the value in the skills and actually be excited about them before you'll use them.

We learn and remember those things that are important to our survival—not only our physical survival, but also our perceived emotional survival, professional survival, and survival in personal relationships. If I believe I need to master new technology to be successful, I have lots of motivation to learn about it.

Larry Squire, a neuropsychologist at the University of California, San Diego, has done an exploration of those components of the brain that process memory and learning. He found that the hippocampus, located in the forebrain, plays a crucial role in cataloging memories. It temporarily records events, then helps store the information in long-term memory. Robert Sylwester, a college professor and researcher at the University of Oregon, believes the hippocampus acts like a librarian, weighing information, cataloging it, and filing it away. If it determines

High motivation is key to learning and using memory skills.

We learn and remember those things that are important to our survival.

the information is valuable, it helps place it in long-term storage in the neo-cortex. If Sylwester's research is true, it's a powerful validation of the importance of discovering personal benefits or the WIIFM (What's In It For Me). Without the WIIFM, the hippocampus never recognizes the importance of certain information, and therefore never helps place that information in long-term memory.

2

When Your Mind
Meets Your WIIFM

You are a born "learning machine." You've been learning new skills since the day you came into this world, and you continue to learn something new every day. Not only are you constantly learning, you're constantly adapting to new information and new situations as they come up. Both of these abilities—learning and adapting—are enhanced by how motivated you are, how emotionally "juiced up" you are about a situation. So if you're going to keep pace with the rapidly changing world, you must not only use your abilities, you must also repeatedly find the motivation to take action.

Let's take a look at your achievements. If you're like most people, you mastered the art of walking when you were about one year old. You stood up, wobbled and fell dozens of times before taking those first steps, but you were motivated to learn to walk. By age two, the desire to discover, interact with and control your environment drove you to learn to communicate through speech. By age five, you had already mastered 90 percent of your adult vocabulary. By age seven you tackled one of the most difficult and complex learning tasks a human being can undertake: you learned to read. Your brain figured out how to associate symbols with sounds, processing them into words in a split second.

During the first years of your life, you were soaking up information and developing skills at an incredible rate. But why? Were you rewarded with a new toy every time you learned a word or mastered a skill? Probably not. What, then, drove you to learn? What motivated you to do so much?

At that age, you were intrinsically motivated to examine every object, explore every new stimulus and take on every new skill—purely to satisfy your hunger to learn. In

The stronger your motivation, the better you remember.

To keep pace with the rapidly changing world:

Use your abilities

::

Repeatedly find the motivation
to take action

short, you learned for the sake of learning. At birth, you had burst into the world with your motivation already in place, and you acted on that motivation from the first moment of your life.

Today, you still need to learn new information at an incredible rate if you're going to stay on top of the changes going on around you. Whether it's taking on new assignments as part of expanded responsibilities at work, or having to learn something new that doesn't come easy—you need new skills and knowledge to keep things running.

Just keeping up with day-to-day changes can be overwhelming. There are newspapers and reports to read; new technology to master, and the constant flow of "new/improved" software programs to be learned or re-learned.

Unfortunately, some of us have negative experiences from school and were labeled "poor learners" or "slow learners." Even if you weren't branded as negatively as that, you may still be carrying around ideas about yourself like, "I can't do math; I read slowly; I hate giving speeches." Sometime during elementary school, many of us lost our craving for knowledge. Our activities were being monitored, judged, and graded. We could pass—or we could fail. After a few failures, we learned to take fewer risks, and as we took fewer risks our learning slowed. Fear of failure replaced the yearn to learn.

The trouble is, when you resist learning, you stop growing, and when that happens you put artificial limitations on what you can accomplish in life. To become a Quantum Learner, you need to change your negative beliefs about your ability to learn into a positive, confident recognition that you can learn anything you need or want to. Recapture the motivation that drove you as a young

To stay on top of changes, you need to learn new information at an incredible rate.

Become a Quantum Learner

by changing your

negative beliefs about learning

into a positive,

confident recognition

that you can learn anything

you want to.

child, and you'll have greater control over your ever-changing world, working and living more effectively.

But how do you recapture your child-like motivation? You're no longer a wide-eyed toddler, driven by a natural hunger to explore a new world. What's going to get you excited about learning? The answer is WIIFM (pronounced WHIFF-EM)—an acronym for *What's In It For Me*. WIIFM is what motivates us to do something; it's the benefit we get from our actions.

Before you do almost anything in your life, you either consciously or subconsciously ask yourself this important question: "What's in it for me?" From the simplest daily task to the monumental life-altering decision, everything has to promise some personal benefit, or you have no motivation to do it. Sometimes the WIIFM is very clear in your mind; other times you have to look for it, or even invent it. Because of the way the human brain works, it's extremely important that you find the WIIFM in every learning situation. And to see why this is so, we need to take a closer look at the miraculous creation called the human brain.

How You Learn: The Mechanics of the Brain

Different parts of your brain control different mental and bodily functions. It's exciting to know that memory, emotions and health are all interrelated parts of your brain—a good reason to keep these three areas of your life in balance. When you're in good emotional and physical health, have strong relationships and communicate well, you're at your peak for learning. When one area is out of balance, it affects how well you learn as well as how well you perform in the other areas.

The hippocampus, a small part of the mid-brain, is the first area to process information, and it plays a crucial role

A part of your brain 'decides' what's important.

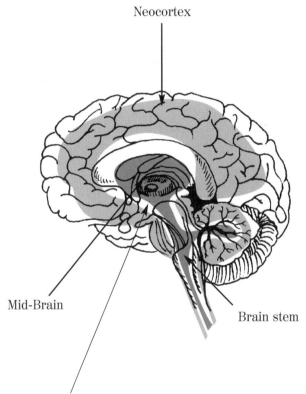

Neocortex

Mid-Brain

Brain stem

Hippocampus

According to neuropsychologist Larry Squire,
the hippocampus temporarily holds information,
while the brain determines if it's important and
valuable, and then stores it in the neocortex in
long-term memory.

in memory. Larry Squire, Ph.D., a neuropsychologist at the University of California, San Diego, has pioneered a systematic exploration of the components of the brain that process memory and learning. According to Squire, when the hippocampus processes facts and events, it temporarily holds the information, while the brain determines if it's important and valuable. If something is important, the hippocampus helps to store it in specific parts of the neocortex for long-term memory. If the information is not deemed valuable, it may soon be forgotten. This is why it's so important to find the value (the "WIIFM") in things we need to learn, so that information will be stored in the neocortex in long-term memory.

The neocortex is an area about the size of a chess board, a quarter-inch thick, that's been "wrinkled up" to fit in your head. This "gray matter" envelopes the lower functioning parts of your brain. The seat of your intellect, the neocortex processes electrical messages. Reasoning, cerebral thinking, decision-making, purposeful behavior and language are found in the neocortex.

The neocortex has left and right hemispheres, with each hemisphere controlling different functions. Although there is cross-over, the left hemisphere is primarily logical, sequential, linear, and rational. Its functions are favored by our society and our school system. Language, writing, reading, math, assimilating details and understanding symbolism are left-hemisphere activities.

The right hemisphere is unordered, intuitive, holistic, and random. It's geared towards non-verbal elements like feelings and emotions, spatial awareness, shape and pattern recognition, music, art, color, creativity, and visualization.

You're a more effective learner when you consciously use both sides of your brain. Yet unless you're an artist,

Include right-hemisphere activities in your heavily left-hemisphere activities to become a more effective learner.

Left	Right
Logical	Emotional
Rational	Intuitive
Sequential	Holistic
Linear	Random/unordered
Detailed	Global/big picture
Language	Music
Writing	Spatial awareness
Reading	Creating
Math	Art

musician, or focus in other highly creative areas, you probably emphasize left-hemisphere activities in school or work. By including right hemisphere activities in your heavily left-hemisphere activities, you'll learn faster, become more intuitive and creative when solving problems, and may even experience sudden flashes of insight.

Quantum Learning employs what are thought of as both left- and right-hemisphere activities, which make learning easier and more rewarding. So as you get caught up in a cycle of continuous growth and improvement, you want to learn more.

- The more you learn, the more you understand.
- The more you understand, the better your decisions are.
- The better your decisions, the more successful you become.
- The more successful you are, the more fun and fulfillment you find in learning . . . and the cycle begins again.

The truth is, we all share the same neurology, stretching back to such famous thinkers as Leonardo da Vinci and Albert Einstein. There are an estimated 100 billion nerve cells in our brains, each with axons and dendrites that connect more strongly with one another when we learn something new. The number of possible connections is—well, mind-boggling. Biologically speaking, we each have the potential to become a genius. In reality, we develop the parts of our brains that we need. When we believe we need to learn something for our survival or interest, we learn it. When we discover benefits for knowing something, we make the effort to know it. Our capacity for learning new things is, for all practical purposes, limitless. So our knowledge and intelligence will increase by our perceived need

Biologically speaking, each of us has the potential to become a genius.

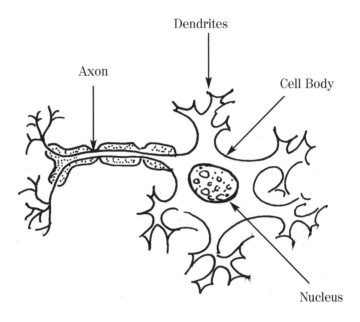

Dendrites

Axon

Cell Body

Nucleus

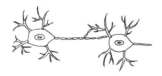

We have an estimated 100 billion nerve cells in our brains, each with an axon that connects more strongly with dendrites from other cells when we learn something new.

to know. Developing a strong desire to do something and perceiving it as a real need is what I call "finding our WIIFM"

In the story on the right, Paulette Thompson discovered her WIIFM—a strong reason to change what she was doing to become more effective. Consequently, she also experienced a shift in how she felt about herself, realizing she had abilities she hadn't known about.

How you feel about yourself spills over into everything you do. When you leave behind the attitude that you can't learn, and remember well, and discover important reasons why you must, you'll find you're empowered with the ability to achieve all you want in life.

Finding Your WIIFM

Everything you do, whether in your professional, school or personal life, must promise some benefit, or you'll have no motivation to do it. Motivation gets you started and keeps you going. There are two types of motivation: extrinsic and intrinsic.

When you're extrinsically motivated, your desire to do something is influenced by someone or something outside yourself. This type of motivation is usually temporary and often negative. It's getting your work done faster so you don't lose your job, or getting a master's degree only to have the initials after your name. Extrinsic motivation is useful in the short term, but has little if any long-lasting effect. You may fall back on extrinsic motivation when you're trying to manipulate others, since it often seems like the easiest and fastest means of reaching your goal.

For example, if you're a sales manager, you may offer a bonus to the salesperson who makes the most sales, or dock the pay of someone who is habitually late. In the

Finding your WIIFM . . .

Paulette Thompson—wife, mother of five, and full-time teacher—rekindled her love of teaching after attending a Quantum Learning seminar. She had been teaching elementary school for 17 years, but was no longer enjoying it.

"When I first started teaching," she later told me over coffee, "I was very energetic. I loved it. But over the years it seemed like schools had changed. Everyone was down on education, and there was little parental support. I got down in the dumps about teaching."

The Quantum Learning seminar, designed especially for educators, gave Paulette new tools for teaching. It also gave her inspiration. "Quantum Learning totally refreshed me. I felt like I did when I first started teaching."

Paulette's new-found enthusiasm affected both her work and her family. Two of her children went to SuperCamp, and her husband started attending Quantum Learning seminars. "My husband is a businessman," she explains. "He buys and sells trust deeds and does a lot of work over the phone. When he saw the change in me and the kids, he wanted to find out what it was all about."

Paulette's WIIFM is the joy she now gets out of teaching, using her new, more effective Quantum Learning methods. Her WIIFM is a renewing force, energizing her every day.

short-term, sales increase and the late employee comes in on time, but once you remove those sources of motivation, both go back to their former state.

Intrinsic motivation comes from inside; it's something that's a part of you, something that makes an activity personally rewarding, interesting and joyful. You do it because you want to. Intrinsic motivation is more likely to stick with you because it's something you want to do for yourself, not something you're doing to satisfy an outside source. If you love school or your work, you probably find it easy to go to there every day. If you're fascinated by new computer programs, you may enjoy learning them and discovering new systems for your company. You do it because you enjoy it.

So what about the things you need to do but don't enjoy? How can you motivate yourself to do them without settling for the short-term extrinsic motivation that eventually loses its appeal?

Asking "What's In It For Me?" can help you discover intrinsic motivation. You'll need to think deeply to get past the extrinsic answers that come up most easily.

Shifting from extrinsic to intrinsic motivation can help with things you know you should do, but keep postponing, like starting a new diet or exercise routine. It may not seem that important, but think back to what I said about health, emotions, and learning all being related. When one of these areas is ignored, it affects the others. You can't do your best work if you're tired, sluggish, have trouble paying attention, or are an emotional time-bomb waiting to go off.

Your extrinsic motivation for diet and exercise might be worrying about what others think of your appearance, fitting into a bathing suit, or meeting others at the health club. In these cases, you're focusing on short term benefits

Intrinsic motivation comes from inside you—it makes an activity personally rewarding, interesting, and joyful.

Asking "What's In It For Me?" can help you discover intrinsic motivation.

and looking for fast results. This kind of thinking has given birth to the many quick weight-loss plans on the market. But because results are short-term and the motivation is extrinsic, dieters are quick to gain the weight back once they get off the plan.

Thinking long-term, you might see eating right and exercising regularly as part of maintaining a healthy lifestyle, something you automatically do every day. You're intrinsically motivated by your desire to be more effective at school or work. The benefits—good health, a clear mind, high energy, and greater self-esteem—boost your performance.

You don't have to be motivated about everything. You can choose what's important to you, and concentrate on those things. You can shift from extrinsic to intrinsic motivation and enjoy long-term results. Remember to ask yourself, "What's In It For Me?"—and you'll discover how a strong motive can unleash the power of your mind and memory.

Focusing on your WIIFM means taking responsibility for your choices.

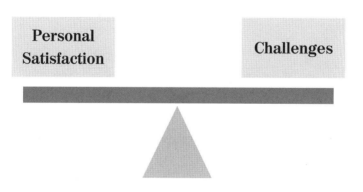

WIIFM can bring enormous personal satisfaction and often also brings challenges.

3

Improve Your Memory
for Fun & Success

Picture yourself enjoying the benefits of a powerful memory. Imagine all the ways you might use it to increase your effectiveness each day.

- The book sitting on your nightstand is one you've been wanting to read for ages, but you haven't had the time. Next time you see it, you remember the specific steps in a speed reading course.
- You have to give a presentation, but instead of practically reading your prepared speech word-for-word, you remember a method you learned for easily recalling your main points and stories . . . in order.

What Would These Kinds of Skills Do for You?

Your job and school aren't the only situations in which you can use good memory skills. It's also fun, not to mention convenient, to memorize numbers like your driver's license, license plate, passport, bank account, PIN, and locker combination. Remembering important phone numbers and dates, like birthdays and anniversaries, can make your life easier and less stressful.

My son Grant was the first to get me excited about the possibilities of memory skills. He learned the skills at a Learning Forum program and uses them more consistently than anyone I know. In high school, his memory skills helped him increase his score on the SAT. He used them to learn 1,600 vocabulary words in one weekend, increasing his verbal score from the 66th percentile to the 99th almost overnight.

Memory skills also helped Grant get his MBA, and he still considers them a valuable tool in his career. As manager of Harry Caray's restaurant in Chicago, he memorized the names of his 165 employees his first week on the job. Then,

Memory skills are valuable in your career, school and personal life.

It's fun and convenient to memorize:

Phone numbers

::

Important dates

::

Driver's license and Social Security numbers

::

Names

::

Sales figures and marketing statistics

::

To-do lists

::

Computer codes, formulas, equations

during a long airplane trip, he memorized over 1,000 food and beverage items along with their assigned accounting numbers. He also uses his memory skills to greatly increase his Spanish vocabulary so that he can communicate with the Spanish-speaking members of his staff. Throughout every day, he builds on and discovers more uses for memory skills.

The best thing about these memory skills is they're fun to practice. It's even more fun to amaze your friends and yourself with your expertise. When Grant and I are riding in a car together, he'll quiz me: "Tell me the code for remembering that license plate. Name all the U.S. presidents, in order."

Years ago when I was in real estate, I experienced my first successes with memory systems. The weekend before taking the real estate broker's exam, I took a cram course that included a presentation by memory expert Arthur Bornstein. In the five days following the class, I was able to memorize 40 pages of notes, word-for-word. On test day, I knew the answers and passed the exam. Then I found many other uses for effective memory skills. Since I was working in San Francisco, I memorized the street names from one end of the city to the other. I spent a lot of time each day driving, and this kept me occupied, as I could practice and test myself as I drove.

I had a strong incentive to learn all of these things. They were necessary for professional survival, at least at some level of consciousness. That was my WIIFM.

The first step in developing memory skills you'll actually use is to start with a commitment. Commit to spending a week practicing these strategies. After a week, they'll come to you effortlessly and will be yours for life.

Commit to practicing your memory skills.

Having a strong incentive elevates your commitment level.

Later in this book, I'll show you how to use your heightened perceptions to create strong associations. But first I want to introduce you to what I call the Easy Eight—eight simple ways to make information more memorable.

4

What We
Remember Most

O ur chances of remembering are best when the information includes more than one of the following eight elements: sensory, intense, emotional, outstanding, survival, personal importance, repetition, and firsts and lasts.

1. Sensory

It may sound simplistic, but the first skill you need to learn is simply to pay attention. Why? Because it's difficult to remember something when you aren't paying attention in the first place.

You create the strongest memories by using a combination of sight, sound, motion, smell, and taste.

> *Sights* — Use color and tones, bright and dark. Explore details. Take enough time to see things clearly in your mind. Memory expert Kevin Trudeau makes this point by telling students: "Look around the room carefully. Observe everything blue. Make a mental note of these things, then close your eyes and picture the room. Now, with your eyes closed, tell me everything you saw that's red."

> *Sounds* — Hear the sound of something whenever possible. I've been working on this skill myself. My lowest learning modality is auditory. I realized this one day as my husband and I drove along with the radio on. Joe was laughing and commenting on the radio program, and I found myself repeatedly asking, "What did they say?" Now I practice listening attentively.

The "Easy Eight" make information more memorable.

Information is best remembered when these elements are used in combination:

1 Sensory

2 Intense

3 Outstanding

4 Emotional

5 Survival

6 Personal Importance

7 Repetition

8 First and Last

Motion — See the items moving together. Also, move as you talk. In giving a speech, if I can't remember the next thing I'm planning to say, it sometimes helps to start walking across the stage; then it comes to me.

Feel — Remembering through touch can also be powerful. Do you remember any phone numbers by physically starting to dial them, feeling the buttons and re-creating the pattern? If someone asks you for the number, you may find it difficult to recall without imagining to dial a phone. That's me with my sister's number. Also retracing our steps helps us remember our thoughts, such as where we left something we're trying to find.

Smells — Imagine the fragrance. Smell can be one of the most powerful memory triggers. For many people, the smell of popcorn triggers images of movie theaters, and a certain perfume revives memories of a forgotten loved one. Smell often triggers more than facts. The emotions and tone of an event can be relived through a powerful olfactory association.

Taste — Imagine what something tastes like, especially strong tastes like lemon or coffee.

Brain theory supports the importance of using all of your senses. For the strongest recall, use as many of the

Pay attention!
It's difficult to remember some-thing when you aren't paying attention in
the first place.

 Observe details

 Listen attentively

 Move your body

 Touch things

 Take in smells

 Be aware of taste

above senses as possible, and in different combinations. Researchers have learned that memory of an object isn't stored whole, but remains where it was when it was first perceived. Dr. Nina Dronkers of the University of California at Davis noted that when we think of a tree, "We know the sound it makes in the wind, the look of the trunk, the shape of a leaf." Each of these details may come from a different place in the brain. "The idea that knowledge is distributed is gaining wide acceptance," according to Dronkers.

Research, as reported in a *New York Times* piece titled "The Brain's Memory System Comes Into Focus," by Philip J. Hilts, finds that the brain is an indexer, organizing information into categories. It breaks information down into components, and stores each component separately. When you recall a creature such as a horse—the texture of its hair, the fact it can run fast, its smell, the sound it makes, and so on—the brain stores these bits of information separately. Another part of the brain takes this information and merges the facts together so that we recognize the whole picture. However this complete picture is not stored permanently.

Dr. Antonio Damasio, author of *Descartes' Error* (Putnam, New York, 1994) says these brain indexes do not contain the memories themselves, only the instructions on how to rekindle many related features and memories associated with them. Damasio created the notion of "convergence zones," or indexes that draw information from elsewhere in the brain.

This explains why it's so important to layer our associations with strong visual images, sounds, smells, touch and motion.

2. Intense

To make your images memorable, make them intense:

Knowledge is distributed. Details come from different places in the brain.

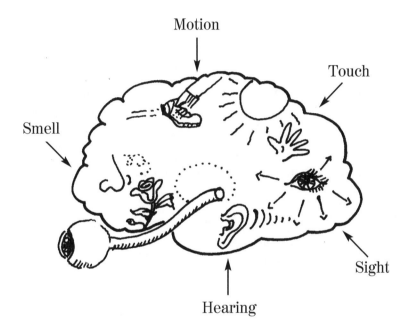

"Convergence" zones draw information together to make complete images.

absurd, sexual, colorful, exaggerated, and imaginative.
For example:

Imaginative sights	— An enormous fly, a tiny elephant, vibrant colors.
Absurd sounds	— Your friend talking like Donald Duck.
Exaggerated movements	— In the old Disney "Flubber" movies, basketball players could jump high above the baskets.

Even though they're intense, be sure to keep your images positive. The mind wants to forget negative and harmful images, so keeping them positive makes them more memorable. If you visualize hitting another person, it should be done in a playful, slapstick style. Avoid harmful intent.

3. Outstanding
Use different qualities, such as all people wearing brown except one person wearing blue. It's not really exaggerated, just different.

4. Emotional
Images charged with love, happiness, and sorrow are easy to remember. Using images of warm feelings, the feelings that make your heart race and bring a glow of happiness, will help your memory and your outlook.

5. Survival
As mentioned previously, a strong WIIFM that's tied to your survival in some area increases your motivation to remember.

Make your images positive.

Keeping images positive makes them more memorable.

6. Personal Importance

Use associations personal to your life such as members of your family, your home, work, friends, events, and things that are special to you.

7. Repetition

Many of us study by repeating something over and over. Some information sticks for a short time, perhaps long enough for us to pass an exam or give a presentation, but we even forget most of that as time passes. Another, more effective way to use repetition is to focus intently on the material and repeat it in different ways such as saying it out loud and making a mind map. Research shows that recall greatly improves if we review information within 24 hours, again in 48 hours, and then in seven days. From then on, with only infrequent reviews, you'll be able to recall the information easily.

8. First and Last

If you were to read a list of items, you'd most likely remember the first thing on the list and the last. When you're introduced to a new group of people, you usually remember best the names of the person you met first and the one you met last. I find, for example, that the opening and closing of a movie will stick in my mind, but I often forget the middle.

To improve your memory, create more firsts and lasts by breaking down information into many small chunks. When you're studying or trying to learn something new, take short, frequent breaks—at least every 30 minutes. This helps you retain more information.

Now you've learned the eight ways people tend to remember best. But how do you remember them? We all

It is recommended information be reviewed within 24 hours, again in 48 hours, and then in 7 days.

Reviewing information at recommended intervals enhances memory recall.

know the characters from the movie, "The Wizard of Oz:" Dorothy, the Wicked Witch, Tin Man, Scarecrow, Cowardly Lion, the Wizard, the Guards, and Auntie Em and Uncle Henry. I will show you how each of these characters may represent one of the eight elements.

1. Sensory

Think of Dorothy as we remember the movie through her eyes. We start by seeing it in black and white—then it switches to color. Imagine what Dorothy sees, hears, smells, and feels.

2. Intense

The Wicked Witch certainly used intense words and motions. Imagine her swirling through the sky, and yelling in her cackly voice.

3. Outstanding

Think of the Scarecrow. He certainly stood out (outstanding) in the field. See him moving and talking.

4. Emotional

Picture the Tin Man yearning for a heart. Then see his huge red heart and hear it pounding.

5. Survival

Picture the Cowardly Lion looking for courage so he could survive in the world. See him quivering with fear.

6. Personal Importance

The Wizard certainly made himself important in the Emerald City.

7. Repetition

Think of the Guards who were always saying, "Oh-ee-oh.

Associate the "Easy Eight" with characters from the Wizard of Oz.

Dorothy

Sensory

We experience
the movie through her

Wicked Witch

Intense

She uses intense
words and motions

Scarecrow

Outstanding

Being distinct from
the others

Tin Man

Emotional

He yearns for a heart

Cowardly Lion

Survival

He's looking for
courage to survive

Wizard

Personal Importance

He made himself
important

The Guards

Repetition

Repetitive in their
musical chants

Auntie Em and Uncle Henry

First and Last

They appear at the
beginning/end of movie

Oh, oh," over and over. Hear the tune from the movie.

8. First and Last

Aunty Em and Uncle Henry only appear at the beginning and the end of the movie. See them worried at the beginning and happy at the end.

Take a moment to review these. Then close your eyes and say the eight elements of a strong memory.

5

Memory Methods & Skills

Imagination and Association

To succeed in remembering, you need to develop a strong, clear, vivid imagination and learn to make strong, clear, vivid associations.

Imagination is the ability to see, hear and sense things in your mind—to create scenes and pictures, both still and moving. For example, picture someplace you know, such as your kitchen. With your eyes open or closed, can you see in your mind what sits on the counter? Where you keep your drinking glasses? Can you picture yourself washing a glass? Can you see that glass dropping and hear it shatter on the floor? Now imagine something you've never seen, like a zebra with orange and green stripes in place of the black and white. Or maybe a dog flying like a bird. Can you see it? That's imagination.

Association is the ability to take one familiar object and connect it with something you're trying to remember. We associate information with sight, sound, smell, and touch. We choose those things most obvious to us personally—the strongest association that comes to mind. No matter what type of association you use, it's important to discover your strongest area, which could be influenced by your learning styles—that is, whether you tend to be more visual, auditory, or kinesthetic.

For most people, the strongest associations are visual. For example, if you wanted to associate objects with numbers, such as the number one and a tree, you could picture the tree trunk as a large number one. To associate the number three to a foot you could picture the three turned sideways. It might look like the toes on your foot. To remember two objects, such as a tree and a chair, you could picture a chair rocking on top of a tree, or a tree growing

Methods for developing a Quantum memory:

Imagination and Association

::

Linking

::

Location

::

Rainbow Strategy

::

Acronyms and Creative Sentences

::

Cues

::

Rote

::

Phonetic Peg System

out of the center of the chair. Get the picture?

To reinforce an image, we can use more than one of our senses. See a picture of a tree, hear the wind through its branches, smell the sweet smells of the blossoms, and feel the texture of its trunk against your skin.

These examples show how you can use associations to memorize concrete things—the stuff you can see, hear, smell, and touch. Other things may not be so obvious. You may even need to invent an association. You'll find examples of memorizing abstract ideas or concepts as we move through this book.

We can also combine sounds with visual images to create associations. Take a word such as "prepare" and hear that "pare" sounds like "pear." Then fit the visual of a pear into your association. In this case, remember to hear the sound of syllables rather than seeing how the words are spelled.

At SuperCamp we teach students to remember things by having them act them out in some small way, creating a movement to go along with what they're trying to remember. For example, the motion for "clear vision" might be moving their hands like a windshield wiper. To "cement a point," they might stamp their feet on the imagined cement floor and pretend the point is written there. We'll teach a list of items, such as U.S. presidents or the mineral hardness scale, through movement, and if students get stuck on an item, we'll say, "Move your body." Even if they don't remember the exact motion, just the act of starting to move their bodies often brings the item to mind.

Linking

Linking is the next most basic memory skill. You can use it to memorize a list by associating each item on the list with the next. It can also be the foundation for other memory strategies. You link things you want to remember and string them together, associating one with another,

Memory skills involve imagination and association.

Imagination –   The ability to see, hear and sense things in your mind

Association –   The ability to take one familiar object and connect it with something you're trying to remember

with another —and on and on.

As an example, here's an easy way to remember the zodiac signs. See a <u>ram</u> (Aries) butting heads with a <u>bull</u> (Taurus). On the bull's back are <u>twins</u> (Gemini), holding a <u>crab</u> (Cancer) because they want to eat it for dinner. The crab is pinching a <u>lion</u>'s (Leo) tail, which causes the lion to roar and break loose. The lion tries attacking a <u>virgin</u> (Virgo), who hits the lion with <u>scales</u> (Libra). She then throws the scales into a patch of <u>scorpions</u> (Scorpio), which get angered and try stinging an <u>archer</u> (Sagittarius), who escapes by jumping on the back of a <u>goat</u> (Capricorn). The goat runs into <u>water</u> (Aquarius), which is filled to over-flow capacity with <u>fish</u> (Pisces), which jump out of the water onto the bank where the ram squashes them while butting heads with the bull, and on and on.

Notice the signs are in order. You probably already know your month and sign and can go forward or backward in the story from there.

Location

Location means associating items sequentially (in order) with specific locations. For example, you can associate a list of items with the parts of your body, starting with the top of your head, then your eyes, nose, mouth, chin, neck, shoulders, and on down to your feet. You can also use the face of a clock and associate things: one item to one o'clock, another to two o'clock, and so on.

One of my favorite location tricks is to associate items with things in my home. To use your home, always imagine the things in your home in the same order as you associate them with items you wish to remember. The order I always use is: the chalk board hanging on my front door, a light switch just inside the door, the entry floor, the living room

The linking method involves stringing items together by associating each item with the next.

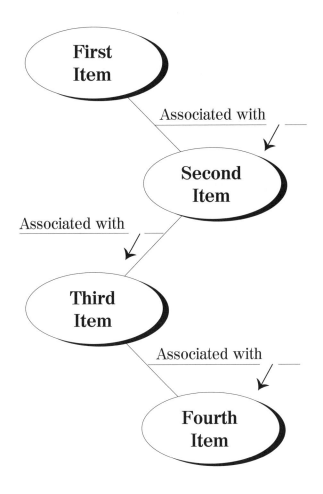

First
Item

Associated with

Second
Item

Associated with

Third
Item

Associated with

Fourth
Item

ceiling, and so on around my home. I use this method most often when I'm giving a speech. As I'm talking to the audience, I can actually visualize myself walking through the rooms remembering items I want to cover by the area of my home I have associated them with.

I imagine my introduction with key words written on the chalkboard. Then I picture the first two points with the two positions of the light switch. I see what I want to say next on the entry floor, and I move on through the entire speech that way. For me this method is very effective; I always know where I am in the speech and what comes next because I can see myself in each room. I suggest you come up with your own list of items using your own home or office. Be sure it's a place you know well and can easily picture in your mind. Attach items in your home to the numbers 1 through 20, in the order you would see these items as you walk through your home. Use the floor-plan on the next page to help you get started.

The Rainbow Strategy

Used in conjunction with location and other methods, this technique helps you keep information in the right sequence. Just follow the colors of the rainbow. See the first set of items in red, the second set in orange, then yellow, green, blue, and purple. This is the order of the rainbow spectrum. This technique is helpful when you use the same set of numbers more than once. I use it with the home location method when I have lots of material and have to walk through my house several times to make all the points. (I'll also show you how to use it for remembering long numbers in the next chapter.)

Suppose you chair five different committees, and you have to brief each one on a new procedure. The informa-

Create a list of 20 items that you see as you move through your home.

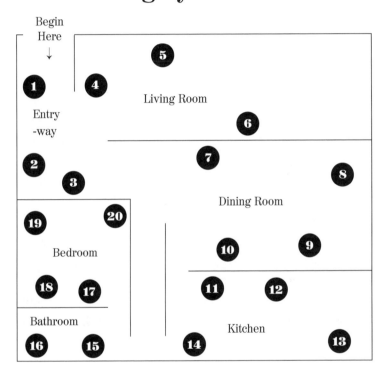

1. _____
2. _____
3. _____
4. _____
5. _____
6. _____
7. _____

8. _____
9. _____
10. _____
11. _____
12. _____
13. _____
14. _____

15. _____
16. _____
17. _____
18. _____
19. _____
20. _____

tion is different for each committee. You'd start by thinking of the first committee as "red," then every item in your house is red when you talk to that committee. The next committee would be orange, and though the items in your house would be the same, the orange color would tell you the information is different. Five committees, five colors of the rainbow.

Acronyms and Creative Sentences

Acronyms take the first letter of several words and create another word. Note that I used the acronym **H.A.T.** to represent **H**ip, **A**bdominal, and **T**high. An acronym you might remember from your school days is **HOMES**, which helps students remember the names of the Great Lakes: **H**uron, **O**ntario, **M**ichigan, **E**rie, and **S**uperior.

Creative Sentences are phrases or sentences using words starting with the same first letter of what you want to remember. If you wanted to remember the order of the colors of the rainbow—Red, Orange, Yellow, Green, Blue, Purple—it could be Run Or You'll Get Behind (the) Parade (of colors). Do you recall how we memorized the notes of the musical scale when we were kids? The lines were the creative sentence: "Every Good Boy Does Fine" (E,G,B,D,F), and the spaces the acronym: FACE.

Cues

We've all heard the old-fashioned idea of tying a string around our finger to remind us of something—this is a cue, and it's not really all that out of date. A cue can be anything that triggers you to remember something. When I find myself rushing out of the office and don't have time to scribble down a note, I'll put something conspicuously out of place on my desk, like placing my phone right in the

The Rainbow Strategy is a handy technique for grouping and ordering information.

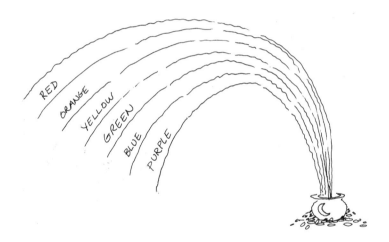

See your images in the colors of the Rainbow.

center. When I come in the next morning, the phone reminds me of what I needed to remember. This is a cue.

Sometimes just beginning a known phrase can help us remember something. A friend of mine was recently trying to remember the name of the Beaver's big brother on the old "Leave It To Beaver" television show. In her mind, she could hear Beaver saying, "Gee, _____. I don't know." But she couldn't fill in the blank with the brother's name. Finally, she said the phrase over and over, trying different names until the name "Wally" popped into her mind. That was it! "Gee, Wally. I don't know."

Rote

Repeating something over and over is probably the least effective way to remember something, but it does work for short-term memorization. You probably have used this method yourself while in school to study for a test.

Acronyms and Creative Sentences are useful memory tools.

Acronym –

Take the first letter of several words
and create another word as in:
- **M** others
- **A** gainst
- **D** runk
- **D** riving

Creative Sentences–

Create a phrase or sentence using words that
start with the same letter of what you want to
remember. As in:

- **R** un **O** r **Y** ou'll **G** et **B** ehind (the) **P** arade

  (**R** ed **O** range **Y** ellow **G** reen **B** lue **P** urple)

6

The Phonetic Peg System

Peg systems are a way of remembering things by associating them with a basic list on numbers and items. The Phonetic Peg System is by far the most powerful of all the peg systems. You can use it for simple associations as well as for complex lists and numbers. Practice will make it easier to use. But be forewarned, you must commit to memorizing the system before you can use it—and that might take you a while. I spent a week learning the numbers and attached items, practicing them as I drove around town. You can practice it anywhere—waiting in lines, or even just lying in bed at night. When I began learning the phonetic peg system, throughout the day, and night, I recited the peg words for numbers I saw. If I awoke during the night, I would glance at my digital clock and mentally say the peg words for the numbers on the clock!

The phonetic peg system uses a list of numbers from 0 to 100. (My own version of it includes 00 through 09, which can be quite useful, as you'll see later.) Each number has a word associated with it. The numbers and words together provide a base to which you then attach or associate what you're trying to remember. You literally hang the information on the pegs.

The phonetic peg system was developed in the 17th century for memorizing lists of any length, order or structure and was highly valued at a time when memorizing stories and information was critical because copying, all of which was done by hand, was costly and time-consuming.

Learning the System

As I said, the phonetic peg system is great for remembering series of numbers, but you can also use it as a general peg system for anything you want to remember. To learn the system, first memorize the consonant or phonetic sounds associated with the numbers 0-9.

Use the Phonetic Peg System for simple associations or more complex lists and numbers.

Commit time and energy to mastering this method:

1 Memorize the phonetic sounds associated with the numbers 0–9.

2 Memorize the word for 0, 10, 20, 30, 40, 50, 60, 70 . . . . This will be your anchor for the next step.

3 Memorize the numbers and words in each group of ten, i.e. 0–9, 10–19, 20–29, 30–39 . . . .

The Phonetic Alphabet

This is both an auditory and visual system, so it's difficult to explain it strictly with words on a page. But I've modified the system to make it easier to learn. You can remember the numbers 0-9 and their attached sounds by using the following associations:

Number		Phonetic Sound	Mental Triggers	
0	=	sa, za ca (soft c)	S0S	– S(Zer0)S
1	=	ma	M1	– M1 rifle
2	=	ra	R2	– R2D2 from Star Wars
3	=	da, ta	3D	– 3 Dimensional 3D glasses
4	=	na	4N	– Foreign
5	=	ja, sha, cha ga (soft g), dg, tch	J5	– Jackson 5, shortened to Ja5 singing Chattanooga Choo Choo
6	=	pa, ba	6P	– 6 pack
7	=	la	7L	– 7-Eleven convenience store
8	=	va, fa, pha ga (hard g)	V8	– V8 juice, Fay Vincent drinking V8 in a Fiat
9	=	ka, ca (hard c)	K9	– Canine, Go, canine

Notice you use the same mouth shape to say the sounds for each number.

Here are mental triggers to help you remember the phonetic alphabet.

0 =   S0S   –   S(Zer0)S

1 =   M1   –   M1 rifle

2 =   R2   –   R2D2

3 =   3D   –   3 Dimensional glasses

4 = **4N**   4N   –   Foreign

5 =   J5   –   Jackson 5

6 =   6P   –   6 pack

7 = **7-ELEVEN**   7L   –   7-E LEVEN

8 = **V8**   V8   –   V8 juice

9 =   K9   –   Canine

The Peg List

To create a peg list, you can come up with words that have the phonetic sounds of the numbers from 0 to 100. Or you can simply memorize the peg list on the right page that my son Grant and I developed. Vowels and the letters H, Q, Y, W, X aren't associated with any number and are used only to complete words, as in HOME, which is a word that conveys the "mmmm" sound. Since 1=M, and the bare "mmmm" sound is not a word, I used the letters H,O and E to create a word that represents the number 1.

As another example, let's look at the first word on the list. For the number zero, the associated sound is s or z. We add vowels and an "H" to create the peg word–in this case "hose." Since the letter H and the vowels O and E don't represent a number, we're left with "S," which is zero. To simplify the memorizing, the list is broken down by tens and the ten words in each group mostly start with the same consonant.

How To Memorize The Peg List

To start memorizing the pegs, create pictures in your mind of the 10 words. This will help you remember a specific series and you can start at any point on the list; you needn't start with one.

For 10, (1=M, 0=S), see a prize moose wearing a big blue ribbon with a number 10 around its neck.

For 20, (2=R, 0=S), see 20 prize rose bushes (a little less than 2 dozen) in the garden. They cost me $20 each!

For 30, (3=D, 0=S/soft C), picture dice with little 30's printed all over them.

For 40, see a nose with a long narrow 40 tattooed on it.

For 50, think of the "Juice Man," a man who's 50 years old and in great shape from drinking juice.

The Phonetic Peg List:

0 Hose	10 Moose	20 Rose	30 Dice	40 Nose	50 Juice
1 Home	11 Mom	21 Ram	31 Dam	41 Name	51 Jam
2 Hair	12 Mare	22 Rear	32 Deer	42 Narrow	52 Jar
3 Hat	13 Mitt	23 Road	33 Dad	43 Net	53 Jet
4 Hen	14 Moon	24 Rain	34 Den	44 Nun	54 Chain
5 Hash	15 Mush	25 Rush	35 Dish	45 Nudge	55 Judge
6 Hobo	16 Map	26 Rope	36 Dip(stick)	46 Nap	56 Ship
7 Hill	17 Mail	27 Rail	37 Dial	47 Nail	57 Shell
8 Hive	18 Movie	28 Reef	38 Dove	48 Navy	58 Chef
9 Hook	19 Mic(rophone)	29 Rake	39 Duck	49 Neck	59 Check

60 Bus	70 Lace	80 Face	90 Case	100 Moses	00 Sauce
61 Beam	71 Lamb	81 Foam	91 Comb		01 Sum
62 Bear	72 Lure	82 Fire	92 Car		02 Soar
63 Bat	73 Light	83 Feet	93 Cat		03 Seat
64 Bone	74 Lion	84 Fan	94 Can		04 Sun
65 Beach	75 Leash	85 Fish	95 Cash		05 Sash
66 Baby	76 Lab	86 Fib	96 Cab		06 Sap
67 Ball	77 Lily	87 File	97 Coal		07 Sail
68 Beef	78 Leaf	88 Fife	98 Cave		08 Safe
69 Bike	79 Lake	89 Fig	99 Cake		09 Sock

For 60, see a 60's type hippie bus.

For 70, see lace with a 70 crocheted in the middle.

For 80, see the face of an 80-year-old woman.

For 90, see a sunglasses case with the designer name 'ninety' imprinted on it

Linking the Pegs

The most difficult part of this system is to initially memorize this list. For me, it helps to link the pegs in a story.

0-9

Start with <u>hose</u> (0). See a hose laid out in the shape of a big circle (like a 0) on your front lawn. See the door of your <u>home</u> shaped like a large #1. Inside is a person with long <u>hair</u>. See her 2 braids sticking up and shaped like R's. See a <u>hat</u> on her head shaped with 3 points sticking up. Then see a very strange <u>hen</u> with 4 legs pulling off the hat and then falling into a plate of <u>hash</u> on the table and walking across it. See the imprint of the hen's 5 toes in the hash. See a <u>hobo</u> (6) sitting on a chair at the table hungrily looking at the hash. The hobo then gets up, as he doesn't like it, and goes outside to walk up a <u>hill</u> (7) where he sees a <u>hive</u> (8) hanging from a <u>hook</u> (9).

Tens

See the <u>moose</u> with the blue ribbon with the 10 around his neck. See <u>Mom</u> standing next to the moose, petting it with her hand. Her other hand is petting a <u>mare</u> that is 12 hands high. This mare is strange . . . it has a <u>mitt</u> on its foot and it looks especially eerie with the <u>moon</u>light shining down on it. The mare walks forward and steps into <u>mush</u> that's laying on top of a <u>map</u>, which shows him what direction to go to <u>mail</u> a letter before seeing a <u>movie</u> where every seat is equipped with a <u>microphone</u>.

A powerful memory requires the ability to visualize what you've trying to remember.

Here's a visual
picture for
remembering
the pegs for 0-9.

0 = hose
1 = home
2 = hair
3 = hat
4 = hen
5 = hash
6 = hobo
7 = hill
8 = hive
9 = hook

Twenties

See 20 prize <u>rose</u>bushes in a garden. A <u>ram</u> charges out of the garden and into the <u>rear</u> of a car that's on a <u>road</u>. Then the <u>rain</u> comes down and the car <u>rush</u>es away. Someone ties a <u>rope</u> to the car to slow it down but it runs onto a <u>rail</u>, which it follows, them it falls into a <u>reef</u> where someone is raking the bottom with a <u>rake</u>.

Thirties

See <u>dice</u> with 30's printed all over them. Throw the dice and see them falling over a <u>dam</u>. At the edge of the water below the dam is a <u>deer</u>, and <u>Dad</u> comes out of the woods to look at the deer. He goes home to sit in his <u>den</u> and eats ice cream off a <u>dish</u> with a <u>dip</u>stick. He then <u>dials</u> his phone and says to the person on the other end, "My goodness, a <u>dove</u> just flew past the window and now a <u>duck</u> is walking by."

Forties

See a <u>nose</u> with a narrow 40 written down it. It's the <u>name</u> of the nose and it's written very <u>narrow</u> because it's a narrow nose. And over the head (and the nose) is a <u>net</u>. It's a <u>nun</u>'s nose and net, and she gives a <u>nudge</u> to someone who's taking a <u>nap</u> on a bed of <u>nails</u>. This someone is in the <u>Navy</u>. I know because he's wearing a uniform. On his <u>neck</u> I notice a tattoo that reads '49'.

Fifties

Think of the "<u>Juice</u> Man," 50 years old and still in great shape from drinking juice. See him sitting at the breakfast table eating <u>jam</u> and juice out of a <u>jar</u>. He runs out the door to catch a <u>jet</u> plane that can't take off as it's held down by <u>chain</u>s. A <u>judge</u> confirms it: "You can't take off." So he leaves by <u>ship</u> and takes a <u>shell</u> from the beach to give to the <u>chef</u> who wrote him a <u>check</u> for his food.

Here's a visual picture for remembering the pegs for 30-39.

30 = Dice
31 = Dam
32 = Deer
33 = Dad
34 = Den
35 = Dish
36 = Dip(stick)
37 = Dial
38 = Dove
39 = Duck

Sixties

See a 60's hippie <u>bus</u>. Light <u>beams</u> are shooting out of the bus. Through the beams you see a <u>bear</u> who runs into a baseball <u>bat</u>, which makes him dizzy. He has a <u>bone</u> in his mouth and he's running and running to the <u>beach</u> where there's a <u>baby</u> playing with a <u>ball</u>. The ball flies up and lands on the <u>beef</u> on a barbecue that has a <u>bike</u> leaning against it.

Seventies

See a beautiful, dainty piece of <u>lace</u> with the number 70 crocheted in the middle of it. This lace is now around the neck of a <u>lamb</u> and pinned together with a fishing <u>lure</u>. The lamb is standing in the bright sun<u>light</u> and is spotted by a <u>lion</u> who runs after it. The lion has a <u>leash</u> around its neck which trails behind as the big cat runs. It runs right up to a <u>lab</u> building with a <u>lily</u> by the front door which has a beautiful <u>leaf</u>. The whole scene reflects on the nearby <u>lake</u>.

Eighties

See the wrinkled <u>face</u> of an 80-year-old woman. In her hand is an extinguisher shooting <u>foam</u> at a <u>fire</u>. Her <u>feet</u> are hot and she's jumping up and down. To cool her feet she holds them up in front of a <u>fan</u>. The fan blows a <u>fish</u> smell that's very unpleasant. A man nearby <u>fibs</u> and says, "There is no fish!" And you can see there is a fish in a <u>file</u> folder. To distract you, he begins to play a <u>fife</u> and offers you a fake <u>fig</u> to eat.

Nineties

See an eyeglasses <u>case</u> with the designer brand "90" imprinted on it. Inside is a <u>comb</u> rather than glasses and the case is sitting on the hood of a <u>car</u>. A <u>cat</u> that's also on the hood wakes up and jumps off the car, landing on a <u>can</u> that turns over and spills out <u>cash</u>. Take the cash and jump

And here's a picture for 60-69:

60 = Bus
61 = Beam
62 = Bear
63 = Bat
64 = Bone
65 = Beach
66 = Baby
67 = Ball
68 = Beef
69 = Bike

in a <u>cab</u> and drive over some <u>coal</u> and into a <u>cave</u>. Inside there's light from the glow of candles on a birthday <u>cake</u>.

00-09

I found it helpful to also have associations for the numbers 00-09 as many phone numbers and other important numbers are made up of these figures. For these lnumbers you can: see a large pot of <u>sauce</u> that includes the <u>sum</u> of all the ingredients. And as you complete adding the ingredients, you see a glider plane <u>soar</u>ing overhead so you take a <u>seat</u> in the <u>sun</u> to watch. You wear a <u>sash</u> across yourself to protect you from the sun and also from the <u>sap</u> that falls from a tree. It's not enough protection, so you cover yourself with a <u>sail</u> and you feel <u>safe</u>. Especially as you also put on a <u>sock</u>.

If you forget a word, you have only to think of the phonetic sound the number represents and usually the word will come to you. If it doesn't, go back to the previous ten (that is, 10, 20, 30, etc.) and repeat the story to yourself. In a second it should come to you. If you still can't think of the word, make up another word that fits with the sound.

Whenever possible, a peg word should be a noun, something you can actually see. Notice in the example above, I said, 'You see a glider plane soaring overhead.' The word is <u>soar</u>, so I added a glider plane (noun)—something you can see. Also, instead of *taking* a seat, *see* a seat (chair/bench). Instead of *feeling* safe, *see* a safe (vault). Instead of a vague sum, see a list of ingredients with plus signs beside them.

Examples of Ways to Use the Phonetic Peg System

You'll find unlimited uses for this peg system. Use it to remember numbers, speeches, facts, "to-do" lists, direc-

Use the Phonetic System frequently and you'll easily remember it.

If you can't remember a word:

Think of the phonetic sound the number represents.

::

Go back to the previous "ten" and repeat the story.

::

Make up another word that fits the sound.

tions, just about anything you want to remember.

For example, I use it to remember how much weight to use on each piece of workout equipment at the gym. I found it awkward carrying around a sheet of paper so I could look up the weight at each station. I solved that problem. Here's how I remember:

• Leg press:	70	Loose	(different than lace but works, $L = 7$ and $S = 0$) I start by imagining my legs getting loose.
• Leg Extensions:	25	Rush	I then rush to the next leg machines.
• Leg Curls:			(same image as leg extensions)
• Chest Press:	20	Rose	I picture a long-stemmed red rose lying across my chest, and know that rose is related to all the upper body machines.
• Shoulder press:	15	Mush	For the shoulder press I have to pump my arms up and down. This is one machine where I picture myself making mush out of the rose.

There are many ways to make use of your phonetic peg system.

You can even use it to remember how much weight to use on workout equipment!

• Lat Pulls:	20	Rose
• Seated Row:	20	Rose
• Hip:	40	I kNowS (N = 4, S = 0) H.A.T. (hip, ab, thigh) is 40
• Abdominal:	40	
• Thigh:	40	
• Glute (buttock):	20	but the butt with the tattooed rose is 20.

These associations are silly and not grammatically correct, but they work. Remember, crazy sights help our recall.

A great application of the phonetic peg system is to use it for remembering phone numbers. For example, take the phone number (320) 478-0082. (By the way, this is no one's number, so don't bother to dial it.)

1. First, associate the numbers with our phonetic words. See 3 = hat, 20 = rose. Picture the person whose number this is, say her name is Jill, wearing a hat decorated with roses.

2. Next, see 4 = hen, 78 = leaf, 00 = sauce, 82 = fire. Then picture a hen running after Jill, so it can eat a rose . . . but really it's the leaf that the hen is after. Jill starts to run and steps into a pot of sauce left cooking over an open fire.

This is nonsensical, but if your images are strong and vivid, it will stay with you. I chose random numbers to illustrate how images that are not logically connected can be linked together.

The Phonetic Peg System is great for remembering all kinds of numbers.

To remember a phone number, or any long number, break it down into groups of one or two numbers, attach the peg word, and order it by using the Rainbow Strategy.

(320) 478-0082

(3	20	) 4	78	- 00	82
red	*orange*	*yellow*	*green*	*blue*	*purple*
hat	rose	hen	leaf	sauce	fire

To help you remember the correct order of the items, use the Rainbow Strategy by seeing them in color. See a red hat, an orange rose, a yellow hen, a green leaf, a blue sauce, and a purple fire.

I've taken groups of phone numbers I want to remember, such as those of our 20 staff members at the office, and written words for each of their numbers. This makes it easier for me to first make the connections and then to review them. I've also listed other personal numbers that I want to remember such as my passport and driver's license numbers, and memorized them all at one time. I write these on an index card that I carry around so that I can easily review the numbers whenever I have a moment, like when waiting in lines.

Cues are triggers to help us remember.

Visual Cues
A string around your finger, or putting something out of place

Auditory Cues
Begin a known phrase or go through the sounds of sounds of the alphabet

7

Let's Practice

Here are some examples of memory techniques you can use to remember Quantum Learning Strategies. If you have not yet learned or read about these strategies, this is good practice for learning new material or random lists

Key Elements to Successful Work Environments

We can remember the key elements in creating successful group environments by using our phonetic peg system. I used the thirties.

30 **Dice** Clear Vision

See yourself walking and wearing an unusual pair of glasses. The lenses are actually a large clear pair of dice, and they provide excellent vision.

31 **Dam** Mission Statement

Picture a Spanish mission sitting near a dam. The water splashes up on you as you sit outside the mission.

32 **Deer** Alignment on Principles and Beliefs

See deer standing in alignment, one after the other. They are highly principled and you can't believe what your eyes are seeing.

Use memory techniques to recall information presented in this book.

Remember the key elements in creating successful group environments:

Clear vision

∷

Mission statement

∷

Alignment on principles and beliefs

∷

Safety and trust

∷

Strong relationships

∷

Visible communication

33 **Dad**	High Level of Safety and Trust	Your Dad provides a high level of safety and trust.
34 **Den**	Strong Relationships	Strong relationships are created when friends gather in the den.
35 **Dish**	Visible Communication	See a huge satellite dish delivering very visible communication to your TV.

Memorizing The 8 Keys of Excellence

Quantum Learning embodies 8 Keys of Excellence. To remember them, use your body by associating each Key to a specific body part.

1. **Head**	Integrity	Palms together over your head. Your body is in the shape of an "I" with Integrity all through it.
2. **Nose**	Failure Leads to Success	You can smell success with your nose.
3. **Mouth**	Speak with Good Purpose	You speak through your mouth and only with good purpose.

To memorize the 8 Keys of Excellence, use your body to associate specific keys with body parts.

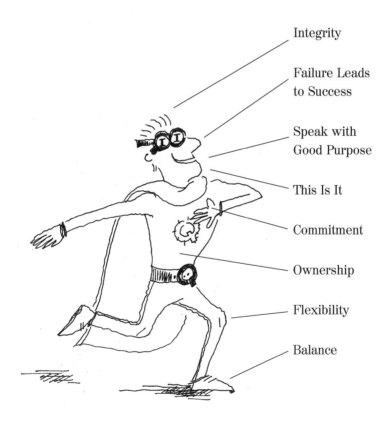

Integrity

Failure Leads to Success

Speak with Good Purpose

This Is It

Commitment

Ownership

Flexibility

Balance

4. **Chin**	This Is It	Always walk with your chin up and have a great attitude about all you do.
5. **Arms**	Commitment	I flex my muscles to show I'm strong and committed.
6. **Stomach**	Ownership	I am what I eat and I take ownership of who I am and of my actions.
7. **Legs**	Flexibility	As I'm highly flexible, my legs can do amazing feats. I'm open to new ideas and changes.
8. **Feet**	Balance	I'm balanced on my feet. My life is about keeping balance in all areas of my life.

The Quantum Reading Process

One way you can remember the Quantum Reading Process is by associating it with major holidays. This list includes the U.S. and Christian holidays that most Americans celebrate. You can substitute holidays that are meaningful to you and your traditions.

| • **Prepare** | Easter/spring | Preparing for a new beginning |

Remember the Quantum Reading process by associating them with major holidays.

Prepare
Easter/spring

::

Get Into State
Fourth of July

::

Use Eye/Hand Skills
Halloween

::

Superscan
Thanksgiving

::

Read
Christmas

::

Review
New Year's Eve

• **Get into State**	Fourth of July	Celebrating the indepen-dence of the United States.
• **Use Eye/Hand Skills**	Halloween	Mask/cos-tume on eyes/hands.
• **Superscan**	Thanksgiving	Think of Supperscan, scanning all the good food.
• **Read**	Christmas	Santa read-ing long lists.
• **Review**	New Year's Eve	When you've completed your year (reading), review your year's events.

Remembering Names

In business and life, remembering names and titles is crucial. The first step to being able to do this is to pay attention when someone tells you his name. If you don't hear it clearly, ask him to repeat it. Then immediately make a

The ability to remember names and titles is a major benefit to you.

Steps to remembering names:

1 Pay attention when someone tells you his name

2 Repeat the name either to yourself or out loud

3 Immediately make a connection:
- Look for an outstanding physical feature
- Associate with clothing or jewelry
- Connect the name to someone else you know with the same name

connection. The easiest way is to associate the person with someone else you know with the same name.

Kevin Trudeau, author of *Mega Memory,* suggests that before you attend a meeting or group session, memorize the name of each person who will be attending, and associate each name with that person's position or where they are from. You'll find it's much easier to remember the names when you finally meet these people. Once you're at the meeting, Trudeau suggests creating an immediate peg for each person before you hear the name, such as "red sweater," "big earrings," and so on, anything that stands out. (Ideally, I like to find a strong physical feature, but clothing works fine.) Later, you'll associate this person with the peg and will remember her name the next time you meet, even though she may be wearing something different. An example would be someone in a striped sweater named Sally. You may see the sweater with wavy lines that look like "S's" or imagine the stripes making alleys down the sweater, and that rhymes with Sally.

You can also create pegs using outstanding physical features, such as protruding ears, a beard, or long eyelashes. Someone with protruding ears named Frank may make you see franks (sausages) coming out of his ears. Make a game out of it. When you meet someone, notice details immediately and see what kind of peg you can create.

Learning Computer Software

You can also use memory techniques to memorize computer commands. When you want to remember that the command "Control-Alt-Delete" reboots your computer, imagine a boot kicking the computer to alter and delete information. You can use the peg system by matching

The number of uses of memory skills is limited only by your imagination.

Challenge yourself

to come up with

additional uses

each week!

numbers. In our software program, Paradox, F1 is Help and our peg for 1 is home. Think of coming <u>home</u> for help. F2 is "Do It" and our peg for 2 is hair. Picture a fancy <u>hair</u> "do". F7 is toggle and our 7 is hill. Think of a <u>hill</u> with a giant toggle on top if it, throwing you from one side to the other. F9 is edit and our 9 is hook. See a tiny <u>hook</u> going over each line, hooking letters and pulling them out of the words. Come up with your own methods for your computer programs.

Now practice applying the memory skills to your own life. There are many ways to remember any list, be it a "to-do" list, a list of key points in a speech, a book, a system or a list of words. Pick the method that is easiest for you to remember.

Experiment with association, pegs, location, and linking, and discover for yourself the value of a powerful memory. You may want to use different systems for different situations, such as location for speeches, association for names, and a combination of phonetic pegs and linking for numbers. It takes an extra effort at first, but keep practicing until the systems become natural for you. Be committed for one week and practice throughout each day. Before long, both you and your friends will be amazed at the power of your memory.

Celebrate Your Learning!

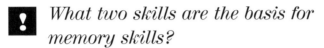

! *Why is having a strong WIIFM especially important to memory?*

It is believed that a part of the brain decides if something is important before it sends it to long-term memory.

! *What two skills are the basis for memory skills?*

A strong, clear, vivid imagination and the ability to make strong, vivid associations.

! *What elements make information more memorable?*

Being highly aware of your senses and thoroughly experiencing your environment makes things more memorable. Creating exaggerated, outrageous, and absurd images with lots of color, action, and vivid detail makes them stick in your mind. Also, tie images to your survival and personal importance, use repetition, and create "firsts and lasts."

! *What are the advantages to learning a memory system, like the Peg List?*

A memory system enables you to remember massive amounts of information with very little effort. And, there's no need to waste time looking up frequently used information. It saves time, reduces stress, and supports your success.

Since 1981, Learning Forum has produced educational programs for students, educators and business. Its vision is to create a shift in how people learn, so that learning will be joyful, challenging, engaging and meaningful.

Programs and products of Learning Forum—

QUANTUM LEARNING PROGRAMS

Quantum Learning is a comprehensive model of effective learning and teaching. Its programs include: **Quantum Learning for Teachers**, professional development programs for educators providing a proven, research-based approach to the design and delivery of curriculum and the teaching of learning and life skills; **Quantum Learning for Students,** programs that help students master powerful learning and life skills; and **Quantum Learning for Business,** working with companies and organizations to shift training and cultural environments to ones that are both nurturing and effective.

SUPERCAMP

The most innovative and unique program of its kind, SuperCamp incorporates proven, leading edge learning methods that help students succeed through the mastery of academic, social and everyday life skills. Programs are held across the U.S. on prestigious college campuses, as well as internationally, for four age levels: Youth Forum (9-11), Junior Forum (12-13), Senior Forum (14-18), and College Forum (18-24).

SUCCESS PRODUCTS

Learning Forum has brought together a collection of books, video/audio tapes and CD's believed to be the most effective for accelerating growth and learning. The *Quantum Learning Resource Catalog* gives the highlights of best educational methods, along with tips and key points. The Student Success Store focuses on learning and life skills.

For information contact:

LEARNING FORUM
1725 South Coast Highway • Oceanside, CA • 92054-5319 • USA
760.722.0072 • 800.285.3276 • Fax 760.722.3507
email: info@learningforum.com • www.learningforum.com

Bobbi DePorter is president of Learning Forum, producing programs for students, teachers, schools and organizations across the US and internationally. She began her career in real estate development and ventured to co-found a school for entrepreneurs called the Burklyn Business School. She studied with Dr. Georgi Lozanov from Bulgaria, father of accelerated learning, and applied his methods to the school with great results. Having two children and seeing a need to teach students *how to* learn, she then applied the techniques to a program for teenagers called SuperCamp, which has now helped thousands of students relearn how they learn and reshape how they live their lives. In addition to SuperCamp, Learning Forum produces Quantum Learning for Teachers staff development programs for schools, and Quantum Learning for Business for organizations. Bobbi is also a past president of the International Alliance for Learning.

She is the author of ten books on the subject of learning. *Quantum Learning: Unleashing the Genius in You, Quantum Teaching: Orchestrating Student Success,* and *Quantum Business: Achieving Success through Quantum Learning* are published in the United States, Great Britain, Germany, Slovenia, Brazil, Russia and Indonesia. These books continue to influence the expansion of Quantum Learning programs and draw international interest.

Mike Hernacki, a former teacher, attorney, and stockbroker, has been a freelance writer and marketing consultant since 1979. He is the author of four books: *The Ultimate Secret to Getting Absolutely Everything You want, The Secret to Conquering Fear, The Forgotten Secret to Phenomenal Success,* and *The Secret to Permanent Prosperity.* His books have been translated into six languages and are sold all over the world. He now divides his time between writing and personal success coaching.